If you've ever wondered why so r   li,
Mom!" when they find themselves (it
role so many moms play in the physical, relational, and spiritual development of their
boys. In fact, Jesus himself acknowledged his mother in the hours before he died.
He knew first-hand the crucial role his own mother played in preparing him for the
miraculous call of God on his life.

Sandee Macgregor has a God-given gift of helping readers zero in on God's
truth for moms and their children. My own mother loved me enough to teach me
God's word, pray for me daily, and lead me to Jesus. She is the reason I'm here
today. Don't miss the opportunity God has given you in helping your boys become
everything God intends for them to be. *Walking in Wisdom Through Proverbs* will
lay a firm foundation of biblical truth for their life, and yours. I highly recommend it!

—**Neil Boron**, Host of Neil Boron Live on WDCX 99.5 FM and 970 AM

What I greatly appreciate about this devotional is that it is thoroughly biblical, entirely
practical, and creatively applicational. It prepares the soil and then provides the seed
of God's word to have the best opportunity to take root and bear fruit in the unique
relationship of a mother and her son. What a necessary and fantastic tool Sandee
has provided for the distracted and confused homes of our day. This devotional
unpacks and applies the desperate need for God's wisdom in each home today. I
enthusiastically recommend it to your family.

—**Robbie Symons**, Senior Pastor, Hope Bible Church (Oakville, Ontario)

Sandee made this devotional to be so Spirit-filled, encouraging, and connective!

—**Tori Hope Peterson**, Author of *Fostered: One Woman's Powerful Story of
Finding Faith and Family in Foster Care*

Our stewardship in having children is to teach about the love of God and the ways of
God, and to instruct and guide and pass on to our children our knowledge of God.
It is a sacred job description God gives to mothers, and Sandee's book on Proverbs
is a wonderful tool for this task. Proverbs instructs us in every area of life, and this
insightful guide is so accessible for opening up the eternal truths to those we love
most.

—**Lorna Dueck**, CEO of The News Forum and Media Consultant

A Devotional for Mothers and Sons: Walking in Wisdom Through Proverbs is a much-needed book today more than ever before. There is a war over the hearts and minds of our sons. This devotional is a gift in preparing our sons with godly wisdom to anchor their hearts and give them a solid foundation for making wise choices in the years to come. It is clear, biblical, and practical. It allows the special bond between a mother and son to strengthen while learning together about the wisdom taught through the book of Proverbs and the truth set out in the Bible.

A mother leaves on her son a lasting imprint. What a beautiful picture of learning together through this special bond. The journaling component is a unique way to communicate from the heart, look back, and remember, to treasure and remind us of all of the wisdom found in Proverbs. Not only are we raising sons but we are also raising future husbands and fathers. This is a must-read devotional for mothers and sons. It is time invested you will never regret.

—**Jeff Gamache**, Athletic Director, Trinity Western University

—**Jennifer Gamache**, Elementary School Teacher

Both are parents to three grown children.

There is something deeply intimate and precious about a mother-son relationship. Sandee Macgregor has captured the depth and essence of those relationships in her latest brilliant devotional. It's the nurturing side of a mother to instil integrity and wisdom into her beloved children, and what better way than to walk with them through the book of Proverbs. Not only is this devotional filled with love and wisdom, the layout of the book allows mothers and sons to engage and connect through discussion and activities that cultivate understanding, rapport and spiritual guidance. This book is a masterly tool to grow the spiritual hearts and minds of the sons who continue to be the heartbeats walking around outside of a mother's body.

—**Heidi McLaughlin**, International speaker and author of *Fresh Joy*

This sweet devotional not only invites us into a deeper relationship with God, but also fosters a beautiful intimacy between mother and son. As you work through the 5-week study of Proverbs with your son, you will encounter God's love and wisdom as you discover fresh ways God works graciously in your lives and hearts through sharing stories of triumph and trial, hopes and challenges with each other.

—**Kellie Haddock**, Songwriter and hope-giver

Sandee Macgregor

A Devotional for
Mothers and Sons:
Walking in Wisdom
through
Proverbs

Published by: Castle Quay Books
Burlington, ON, Canada | Jupiter, FL, USA
Tel: (416) 573-3249
E-mail: info@castlequaybooks.com | www.castlequaybooks.com

Edited by Marina Hofman Willard
Cover design and Book interior by Burst Impressions
Printed in Canada

Library and Archives Canada Cataloguing in Publication
Title: A devotional for mothers and sons : walking in wisdom through proverbs / by Sandee Glo Macgregor.
Names: Macgregor, Sandee G., author.
Identifiers: Canadiana 20220262160 | ISBN 9781988928647 (softcover)
Subjects: LCSH: Bible. Proverbs—Devotional literature. | LCSH: Sons—Religious life. | LCSH: Mothers—
Religious life. | LCSH: Mothers and sons—Religious aspects—Christianity. | LCSH: Spiritual journals—Authorship.
Classification: LCC BS1465.54 .M337 2022 | DDC 242/.5—dc23

CASTLE QUAY BOOKS

Sandee Macgregor

 is the creator and founder of the website and blog Sovereign Radiance, a hope-filled place that provides a connection with like-minded moms as we travel the journey of parenting together. She is the award-winning author of *A Mother-Daughter and Shared Journal Experience for Psalm 119*, which encourages a deeper spiritual connection between moms and daughters through reading daily passages, praying, memorizing, and journaling together. Sandee is educated and trained as a teacher and has homeschooled her children over the past fifteen years. She continues to pursue her love of writing and reading while living in the country, enjoying long walks with her dogs and celebrating life with family and friends around the dinner table. She is a follower of Christ, wife to Duncan for twenty-six years, and a mom to five children. To learn more about Sandee and to follow her on the journey into the heart of motherhood, visit her at www.sandeemacgregor.com.

Dedication

Thank you to godly sons who did (and still do) lean into wisdom from their moms and influenced future generations.

My dad, Gerry

My grandfathers, Harold and Mel

My father-in-law, Duncan Sr.

My husband, Duncan Jr.

My brother, Burke

My brothers-in-law, Mark and Gord

To my boys, Chris and Jack:

May you always hear the call of wisdom.

I am proud to be your mom.

I love you.

For you: Isaiah 43:2, Exodus 14:14.

To my girls, Samantha, Sara, and Katie:

You have helped me become a better mom to your brothers; thank you.

For you: Psalm 119:130.

CONTENTS

A Note from My Dad, Gerry Mudge

It is an honour and blessing to comment on this book for mothers and sons by my daughter, Sandee. While the relationship between mothers and daughters is very special, it is also true that sons love their mothers. As a son and father, I am very grateful for the relationship with my mother. Godly women throughout history have influenced their sons to become exceptional leaders and influential people in history.

Sandee and her husband, Duncan, are always working together to raise their family, relying on strength from God. In this devotional, she encourages a mother's relationship with her son and emphasizes the importance of Scripture application through Proverbs.

May this book encourage moms to build into their unique sons' lives.

I love you and am proud of you.

Your Dad

A Note for My Dad, a Trusted Guide

Dear Dad,

You have demonstrated a love for Jesus that changed my life. Wisely, you leaned into my moments and days and allowed God's Word to rest in my heart, even when I resisted. You actively chose to create these moments because you met Jesus and desired to show us his love. It was your care and service to our family that helped us keep Christ at the center of our lives. Gently, you guided our understanding of a personal relationship with Jesus in three simple and effective ways: you opened the Bible, prayed, and brought us to church. This was a chosen way of laying a foundation for my future and our family. You built our house on a rock, not sinking sand.

> "Therefore everyone who hears these words of mine and puts them into practice is like a wise man who built his house on the rock. The rain came down, the streams rose, and the winds blew and beat against that house; yet it did not fall, because it had its foundation on the rock." (Matthew 7:24–25)

Dad, you intentionally provided biblical tools for me to build upon. As I walk my path, I gratefully gather these truths I can share with my children, no matter their ages. You listened to wisdom respectfully from your mom and cherished her; that is a gift I hold fast to and desire to share with your grandsons. Thank you for leading, loving, and providing.

Your Grateful Daughter

Dear Mother

The battle for our sons' hearts begins early. We hope to see our sons exhibit traits like courage, honour, strength, compassion, and love. Then hopelessness enters without notice and taps us on the shoulder as if to whisper that it's impossible to raise our sons when the world is waging war for their souls.

Remember, God has called us to this role, and he will equip us for the task. Our sons are on loan to us. They belong to God first, which frees us to rest confidently on the rock-solid and ever-present truth that our sons are his and always have been: "I have summoned you by name; you are mine" (Isaiah 43:1). Knowing this truth ourselves enables us to regularly impress this on the hearts of our sons. Clothed with the armour of God (Ephesians 6:10–20), we can stand firm, undergirded with the most powerful protection through prayer.

Motherhood, at times, can feel lonely, with a never-ending "perfect" son checklist to present before the world. It is tempting to rely on our strength as we raise our sons. Psalm 121:1–2 encourages us where to look, "I lift up my eyes to the mountains—where does my help come from? My help comes from the Lord, the Maker of heaven and earth." With our eyes up, hands raised, and knees bent in surrender to Christ, we open ourselves to his will. God's Word calls us to "Cast all your anxiety on him [God] because he cares for you" (1 Peter 5:7) and "Be strong and courageous … for the Lord your God goes with you; he will never leave you nor forsake you" (Deuteronomy 31:6). Be encouraged with the truth from God's Word that provides much-needed direction, hope, encouragement, and love.

Our homes all have a unique God-given style, casting a fragrance of grace imprinted by our Maker. God created us with purpose and uniqueness as mothers! We have an opportunity to bring up our sons in our homes as an offering to him. Without wisdom from the Word of God, we are prone to run after our heart's desires and leave our parenting to the cultural winds. The gift of studying Proverbs is "for gaining wisdom and instruction; for understanding words of insight" (Proverbs 1:2). Proverbs is our manual of grace to embrace and unfold to our sons.

I pray that this devotional and journal creates many meaningful moments. May you and your sons cherish this written record of your hope-filled journey through Proverbs together for years to come.

Using This Devotional and Journal

Each week begins with a **Dear Mom** section that provides a special encouragement for you. There are passages to read daily and a section of verses to focus on, a key verse, prayer prompt, and weekly memory verse. At the end of each day, engage in the **Shared Journal Experience** together. Here, you connect with your sons, writing encouraging words to one another. Inspired by my parents' tradition of writing meaningful notes to their children, I encourage mothers and sons to write one another often. Communicating thoughtfully and creatively can inspire the hearts of our loved ones. Words are vessels the Lord has chosen to speak to us. The time it takes to write a simple note is worth the encouragement your sons will receive. The NIV translation is provided; you may wish to examine other translations of Proverbs for increased understanding.

Allow for extra time on day 5 for **Ready, Set, Go** moments. This is an opportunity for engaging in various activities together, listening to worship music, and exploring suggested books, movies, and audio.

When the Shared Journal Experience is complete, look back and discover what you have learned and how you have grown closer together! May this journal provide you with memorable words to reflect on with gratitude.

Go ahead, inspire the heart of your son!

Part 1
Devotional

Visionary –
The Call of Wisdom

Proverbs 1 and 2

Memory Verse

The fear of the Lord is the beginning of knowledge,
but fools despise wisdom and instruction.
(Proverbs 1:7)

Who am I to tell of your infinite wisdom but by your grace,
and grace alone?

Dear Mom,

My childhood home on the west coast of B.C. allowed me the delight of playing in the ocean for hours. Exploring the tide pools bustling with creatures and endless crab hunting along with the salty breeze are etched in my memory. On one of these adventures, I was barefoot and unaware of what encased the rocks I was about to explore. I tumbled into a mess of barnacles. The sharp edges cut deep like a knife. The playful moments on the seaside became a journey of pain, fear, and panic. Tears ran down my cheeks as my dad immediately carried me to safety.

After a while, I saw the look of concern in my dad's eyes. His being a pharmacist by trade and multiple medical experiences on the mission field in Africa equipped him to see what was happening. A red line spread from my foot creeping dangerously up my leg. My dad understood it was beyond his capabilities and wisely pursued medical attention. Off we went to the hospital and discovered the wound had become infected. I recall the determination in my dad's eyes. I had no idea what was going on or what was just about to happen. Freezing the area was necessary, which meant the doctor administered a needle into my foot. My dad held me down and had to let me scream, cry, and wrestle. If he had not made the decision to seek medical attention quickly, the effect of blood poisoning would have had more serious consequences. My dad did not want me in pain. He knew ultimately that this would bring necessary relief and healing, but not without difficulties. The decision made was wise and accompanied by love for his daughter.

Our heavenly Father's love for us is even more grand and trustworthy through all the trials we experience, he pours it generously out *just for us*, "For great is his love toward us, and the faithfulness of the LORD endures forever. Praise the LORD" (Psalm 117:2). Occasionally, our sons may step on something sharp on a path leading to a painful detour. Alone, this is a challenging burden to bear. Our sons need us by their side and on our knees in prayer seeking godly wisdom.

Verse by verse, Proverbs wisely teaches us how to construct our spiritual houses. The warnings and instructions are for our good, and help us lean into the goodness of our God. In 2 Timothy 2:7, Paul encourages Timothy, "Reflect on what I am saying, for the Lord will give you insight into all this." Even if it takes years for the truth to resonate, we have a tremendous opportunity to do the same with our sons: teach them to reflect and trust in the Word of God. Remember, the words we share and the time we spend with our sons are not wasted. "Therefore, my dear brothers and sisters, stand firm. Let nothing move you. Always give yourselves fully to the work of the Lord, because you know that your labor in the Lord is not in vain" (1 Corinthians 15:58).

Our sons belong to the same God to whom we belong. So, dear mom, hold fast to his Word and pray without ceasing (1 Thessalonians 5:17). You can trust that God will carry your son as he has carried you, for his timing is always perfect.

Day 1

Read and discuss Proverbs 1:1–7.

Purpose and Theme

¹ The proverbs of Solomon son of David, king of Israel:
² for **gaining wisdom** and **instruction**;
    for understanding words of insight;
³ for receiving **instruction** in prudent **behavior**,
    doing what is **right** and **just** and **fair**;
⁴ for giving prudence to those who are **simple**,
    knowledge and discretion to the **young**—
⁵ **let the wise listen** and add to their **learning**,
    and let the discerning **get guidance**—
⁶ for **understanding proverbs and parables**,
    the sayings and riddles of the wise
⁷ The **fear of the Lᴏʀᴅ** is the beginning of knowledge,
    but **fools despise wisdom and instruction**.

Discuss each of the highlighted words and phrases in this passage that lead us toward the call of wisdom. How can these phrases apply to our daily lives? How can we begin right now to gain wisdom and discernment?

Today's key verse: "Let the wise listen and add to their learning, and let the discerning get guidance" (Proverbs 1:5).

Pray together: Lord, we pray for the ability to listen to you so we will have greater discernment in our lives.

Weekly memory verse: "The fear of the Lᴏʀᴅ is the beginning of knowledge, but fools despise wisdom and instruction" (Proverbs 1:7).

Shared Journal Experience: Turn to the Shared Journal Experience for week 1, day 1, and share words of encouragement with each other.

SHARED JOURNAL EXPERIENCE

Week 1. Day 1

Write the start date of your journey: _____

Mom

What do you hope for on this journey with your son? Share a verse from Proverbs and why it is meaningful to you.

_____

_____

_____

_____

_____

_____

_____

_____

_____

_____

_____

_____

_____

_____

_____

_____

_____

_____

MEMORY VERSE

The fear of the LORD is the beginning of knowledge,
but fools despise wisdom and instruction.

(Proverbs 1:7)

SHARED JOURNAL EXPERIENCE

Week 1. Day 1

Write the start date of your journey: _____

Son

What do you hope to learn on this journey through Proverbs with your mom? Write down a word to encourage your mom and share why.

_____
_____
_____
_____
_____
_____
_____
_____
_____
_____
_____
_____
_____
_____
_____
_____
_____
_____
_____

TODAY'S KEY VERSE

Let the wise listen and add to their learning,
and let the discerning get guidance.

(Proverbs 1:5)

WEEK 1

Day 2

Read together Proverbs 1:8–19.
Focus on and discuss Proverbs 1:8–15.

⁸ **Listen**, my son, to your **father's instruction**
and do not **forsake** your **mother's teaching**.
⁹ They are a **garland to grace** your head
and a chain to adorn your neck.
¹⁰ My son, if **sinful** men **entice** you,
do not give in to them.
¹¹ If they say, "Come along with us;
let's **lie in wait** for innocent blood,
let's ambush some harmless soul;
¹² let's swallow them alive, like the grave,
and whole, like those who go down to the pit;
¹³ we will get **all sorts of valuable things**
and fill our houses with plunder;
¹⁴ cast lots with us;
we will all share the loot"—
¹⁵ my son, **do not go along with them,
do not set foot on their paths**.

Discuss each of the highlighted words and phrases in this passage that lead us toward the call of wisdom. How can these phrases apply to our daily lives? How can we begin right now to gain wisdom and discernment?

Today's key verse: "Listen, my son, to your father's instruction and do not forsake your mother's teaching" (Proverbs 1:8).

Pray together: Lord, we pray that your Word would be a garland of grace in our lives.

Weekly memory verse: "The fear of the Lord is the beginning of knowledge, but fools despise wisdom and instruction" (Proverbs 1:7).

Shared Journal Experience: Turn to the Shared Journal Experience for week 1, day 2, and share words of encouragement with each other.

SHARED JOURNAL EXPERIENCE

Week 1. Day 2

Mom

Share a challenging path you took in life and the lessons you learned. Invite your son to share what he thought you may have discovered first, then share your story.

_____

_____

_____

_____

_____

_____

_____

_____

_____

_____

_____

_____

_____

_____

_____

_____

_____

_____

_____

_____

_____

_____

MEMORY VERSE

*The fear of the LORD is the beginning of knowledge,
but fools despise wisdom and instruction.*

(Proverbs 1:7)

SHARED JOURNAL EXPERIENCE

Week 1, Day 2

Son

Have you ever taken a path that caused a trial in your life? Share what you learned. Have you ever taken a wise path? What is the difference between a wise path and a foolish path? Ask your mom for her thoughts.

_____

_____

_____

_____

_____

_____

_____

_____

_____

_____

_____

_____

_____

_____

_____

_____

_____

_____

_____

_____

_____

TODAY'S KEY VERSE

_Listen, my son, to your father's instruction
and do not forsake your mother's teaching._

(Proverbs 1:8)

WEEK 1

Day 3

Read together Proverbs 1:20–33.
Focus on and discuss Proverbs 1:20–27.

²⁰ Out in the open **wisdom calls aloud**,
   she raises her voice in the public square;
²¹ on top of the wall **she cries out**,
   at the city gate **she makes her speech**:
²² "How long will **you who are simple** love your simple ways?
   How long will **mockers** delight in mockery
   and **fools hate knowledge**?
²³ **Repent** at my rebuke!
   Then I will **pour out my thoughts** to you,
   I will make known to you my teachings.
²⁴ But since you **refuse to listen** when I call
   and **no one pays attention** when I stretch out my hand,
²⁵ since you disregard all **my advice**
   and do not accept my rebuke,
²⁶ I in turn will laugh when **disaster strikes** you;
   I will mock when calamity overtakes you—
²⁷ when calamity overtakes you like a storm,
   when **disaster** sweeps over you like a whirlwind,
   when distress and **trouble overwhelm you**."

Discuss each of the highlighted words and phrases in this passage that lead us toward the call of wisdom. How can those phrases apply to our daily lives? How can we begin right now to gain wisdom and discernment?

Today's key verse: "Whoever listens to me will live in safety and be at ease, without fear of harm" (Proverbs 1:33).

Pray together: Lord, we pray you would help us pay attention to wisdom from your Word and live without fear.

Weekly memory verse: "The fear of the Lᴏʀᴅ is the beginning of knowledge, but fools despise wisdom and instruction" (Proverbs 1:7).

Shared Journal Experience: Turn to the Shared Journal Experience for week 1, day 3, and share words of encouragement with each other.

SHARED JOURNAL EXPERIENCE

Week 1, Day 3

Mom

Talk about a time when you listened to God's Word. How did listening to God impact your life?

_____

_____

_____

_____

_____

_____

_____

_____

_____

_____

_____

_____

_____

_____

_____

_____

_____

_____

_____

_____

_____

MEMORY VERSE

The fear of the LORD is the beginning of knowledge,
but fools despise wisdom and instruction.

(Proverbs 1:7)

SHARED JOURNAL EXPERIENCE

Week 1, Day 3

Son

What verse have you read in Proverbs today that gave you peace? Ask your mom the same question, and talk about what that means to daily life.

_____

_____

_____

_____

_____

_____

_____

_____

_____

_____

_____

_____

_____

_____

_____

_____

_____

_____

_____

TODAY'S KEY VERSE

*Whoever listens to me will live in safety
and be at ease, without fear of harm.*

(Proverbs 1:33)

WEEK 1

Day 4

Read together Proverbs 2:1–15.
Focus on and discuss Proverbs 2:1–8.

Moral Benefits of Wisdom

2 My son, if you **accept my words**
    and **store up my commands** within you,
² **turning your ear to wisdom**
    and **applying your heart to understanding**—
³ indeed, if you **call out** for **insight**
    and **cry aloud** for understanding,
⁴ and if you **look for it as for silver**
    and **search** for it as for **hidden treasure**,
⁵ then you will **understand** the **fear of the Lᴏʀᴅ**
    and find the **knowledge of God**.
⁶ For **the Lᴏʀᴅ** gives wisdom;
    from his mouth come knowledge and understanding.
⁷ He holds success in store for the **upright**,
    he is a **shield** to those whose **walk is blameless**,
⁸ for he **guards** the course of the **just**
    and **protects** the way of his **faithful** ones.

Discuss each of the highlighted words and phrases in this passage that lead us toward the call of wisdom. How can these phrases apply to our daily lives? How can we begin right now to gain wisdom and discernment?

Today's key verse: "The Lᴏʀᴅ gives wisdom; from his mouth come knowledge and understanding" (Proverbs 2:6).

Pray together: Lord, give us wisdom in our lives to make decisions with knowledge and understanding that comes from God.

Weekly memory verse: "The fear of the Lᴏʀᴅ is the beginning of knowledge, but fools despise wisdom and instruction" (Proverbs 1:7).

Shared Journal Experience: Turn to the Shared Journal Experience for week 1, day 4, and share words of encouragement with each other.

SHARED JOURNAL EXPERIENCE

Week 1, Day 4

Mom

Share with your son how you have found wisdom through other people in your life.

_____

_____

_____

_____

_____

_____

_____

_____

_____

_____

_____

_____

_____

_____

_____

_____

_____

_____

_____

_____

_____

_____

_____

_____

MEMORY VERSE

The fear of the LORD is the beginning of knowledge,
but fools despise wisdom and instruction.

(Proverbs 1:7)

SHARED JOURNAL EXPERIENCE

Week 1, Day 4

Son

What have you heard your mom say that is wise? Share a time when you made a smart choice.

_____

_____

_____

_____

_____

_____

_____

_____

_____

_____

_____

_____

_____

_____

_____

_____

_____

_____

_____

_____

_____

_____

_____

TODAY'S KEY VERSE

The LORD gives wisdom; from his mouth come knowledge and understanding.

(Proverbs 2:6)

WEEK 1

Day 5

Read and discuss Proverbs 2:16–22.

¹⁶ **Wisdom will save** you also from the adulterous woman,
from the **wayward** woman with her seductive words,
¹⁷ who has left the partner of her **youth**
and **ignored** the **covenant she made before God**.
¹⁸ Surely her house **leads down to death**
and her paths to the spirits of the **dead**.
¹⁹ None who go to her return
or attain the **paths of life**.
²⁰ Thus you will **walk in the ways of the good**
and keep to the **paths of the righteous**.
²¹ For the **upright** will live in the land,
and the **blameless** will remain in it;
²² but the **wicked** will be cut off from the land,
and the **unfaithful** will be torn from it.

Discuss each of the highlighted words and phrases in this passage that lead us toward the call of wisdom. How can these phrases apply to our daily lives? How can we begin right now to gain wisdom and discernment?

Today's key verse: "Thus you will walk in the ways of the good and keep to the paths of the righteous" (Proverbs 2:20).

Pray together: Show us, Lord, how to faithfully walk in your ways and stay on the path of the righteous.

Weekly memory verse: "The fear of the Lᴏʀᴅ is the beginning of knowledge, but fools despise wisdom and instruction" (Proverbs 1:7).

Shared Journal Experience: Turn to the Shared Journal Experience section for week 1, day 5, and share words of encouragement with each other.

SHARED JOURNAL EXPERIENCE

Week 1, Day 5

Mom

Who have you seen faithfully walk with God? How has your son kept the path of righteousness?

_____

_____

_____

_____

_____

_____

_____

_____

_____

_____

_____

_____

_____

_____

_____

_____

_____

_____

_____

_____

MEMORY VERSE

*The fear of the LORD is the beginning of knowledge,
but fools despise wisdom and instruction.*

(Proverbs 1:7)

SHARED JOURNAL EXPERIENCE

Week 1, Day 5

Son

What does it mean to be faithful? How has your mom shown you what it means to walk with Jesus?

_____

_____

_____

_____

_____

_____

_____

_____

_____

_____

_____

_____

_____

_____

_____

_____

_____

_____

_____

_____

_____

TODAY'S KEY VERSE

You will walk in the ways of the good and keep to the paths of the righteous.

(Proverbs 2:20)

Day 5 – Ready, Set, Go

READY to be together

Today, you and your son will embark on creating a treasure hunt! Mom, you can copy the weekly Bible verses written at the bottom of this page and hide them inside or outside along with a treat of choice. Then, your son can create a treasure hunt for you. Get creative and try it again with others!

SET your worship music today

"My Worth Is Not in What I Own (At The Cross)" (Keith and Krysten Getty and We Are Messengers)

"Almost Home" (Mercy Me)

"Lose My Soul (Afterparty Interlude)" (TobyMac featuring Kirk Franklin and Mandisa)

"Every Hour" (David Leonard)

"Talking to Jesus" (Elevation Worship and Maverick City)

GO to read or listen to audiobooks or watch movies together

Listen or watch

"iBible" (Revelation Media)

"Facing the Giants" (Kendrick Brothers)

"The Legend of Squanto" (Focus on the Family Radio Theatre)

Read with your son

"Devotions for Animal Lovers" (Dandi Daley Mackall)

"The 10 Minute Bible Journey" (Dale Mason)

"Ten Boys that Changed the World" (Irene Howat)

"Ten Girls that Changed the World" (Irene Howat)

Books for mom

Missional Motherhood (Gloria Furman)

The Gospel Comes with a House Key (Rosaria Butterfield)

Weekly key verses from week 1 to use for the treasure hunt

Day 1: "Let the wise listen and add to their learning, and let the discerning get guidance" (Proverbs 1:5)

Day 2: "Listen, my son, to your father's instruction and do not forsake your mother's teaching" (Proverbs 1:8).

Day 3: "Whoever listens to me will live in safety and be at ease, without fear of harm" (Proverbs 1:33).

Day 4: "For the Lord gives wisdom; from his mouth come knowledge and understanding" (Proverbs 2:6).

Day 5: "You will walk in the ways of the good and keep to the paths of the righteous" (Proverbs 2:20).

Leader – The Blessings of Finding Wisdom

Proverbs 3 and 4

Memory Verse

Trust in the LORD with all your heart
and lean not on your own understanding;
in all your ways submit to him,
and he will make your paths straight.
(Proverbs 3:5–6)

Changing our son's heart is not our responsibility; it's teaching God's love and faithfulness. Their heart belongs to him.

Dear Mom,

Memories of road trips to visit my grandparents began in our yellow station wagon. After the long, crowded drive, the familiar covered porch was a welcoming view and announced we had finally arrived at Sun Glo Valley Farm. As we rounded the last part of the gravel driveway, whatever dog was on guard barked until it seemed the dog was floating in the air held only by a simple chain. Fortunately, the dog stayed within the confines of the fence purely to protect the nervous grandchildren.

My childhood is filled with countless memories of imaginative summer days on the farm. Life was hard for them, they lived at the mercy of the weather and the threat of inconsistent machinery, financial pressures, and unwanted critters. For the grandchildren, it was prairie paradise waiting to be discovered.

One morning, the discussion of unwanted critters in the barn was a hot topic: what to do with the pigeons? There was a nesting issue in the barn. Farmers often call in the neighbours and family to tackle problems and solve the issue together; we were the collective that morning! I was eager to be involved; it meant I could walk through the barns side-by-side with my dad and grandpa.

Mystery and intrigue awaited. The barn was full of history, and I might hear a story from long ago or uncover something unusual. Walking up the ramp and then entering through the double red doors allowed my mind to imagine what life was like when the barn was bustling with activity. The sun filtered through the barn boards allowing just enough light to enter. The lightbulbs lilted side-to-side and let off a dim hue. The stalls were empty, except for the shadows of the cattle and horses that used to provide milk and a solid day's work.

I was oblivious to the plan to dispose of the pigeons. The moment we climbed the stairs, the first nest in view was quickly discarded. One after another, the nests were removed until I couldn't handle this type of pest control anymore. I devised a plan: find a nest and rescue a baby pigeon. I knew my dad and grandpa were on a mission from the concern in their voices, but now I was too. I found a baby pigeon and carried it for hours hidden in the front pocket of my hoodie for warmth.

Eventually, I went back to the house, and it wasn't too long before my grandma called me over; she had noticed something unusual. She put her knitting aside and asked what I was holding. I wanted to lie. I had no intention of revealing the rescued baby pigeon. But I did. I took the baby pigeon outside and surrendered my secret. I cried. My dad and grandpa knew better, as pigeons were known to overrun barns and be a nuisance. I had to trust them to lead, even if their wisdom was foreign to me.

My dad and grandpa's decision was beyond my childlike version of common sense. I intended to go back into the barn and continue my life-saving efforts, not knowing that I would actually be causing my rescued pets more harm by taking them out of their nest. After my initial loss, I calculated the cost and did not go back to the barn, except to play with my siblings or visit Cindy, the last horse lucky enough to walk the pastures.

Trusting in the wisdom and leadership of my dad and grandpa was an exercise in not being wise in my own eyes. Proverbs 3:7–8 speaks clearly, "Do not be wise in your own eyes; fear the L ORD and shun evil. This will bring health to your body and nourishment to your bones." Giving up my pigeon was not refreshing. But I eventually chose to obey even though my spirit wasn't willing. Foolishness comes at a cost, but listening to wisdom is priceless.

My dad began teaching me the importance of wisdom long before I fully understood the purpose. His ability to make moment-to-moment decisions came from experience, reading the Word, and accountability in his life. Our sons may listen to our teaching, but inside they are often having a spirited debate and perhaps a hardened heart. When we suspect this is happening, it is worthy of our time and effort to ask questions, find the root of the unwillingness to obey, and lovingly point them to our heavenly Father, the One willing to help our rebel nature through his work on the cross.

We share wisdom as best we can with our sons, and allow the Holy Spirit to direct the path they take and shape their hearts. To accomplish this, we must have faith, "Truly I tell you, if you have faith as small as a mustard seed, you can say to this mountain, 'Move from here to there,' and it will move. Nothing will be impossible for you" (Matthew 17:20). The Lord knows the hearts of our sons, and we have the privilege to pray they learn the value of wisdom and listen to the Holy Spirit's leading so they will find strength in their daily lives.

Day 1

Read and discuss Proverbs 3:1–6.

Wisdom Bestows Well-Being

3 My son, **do not forget** my **teaching**,
   but **keep my commands** in your **heart**,
² for they will **prolong your life** many years
   and bring you **peace** and prosperity.
³ Let **love** and **faithfulness never leave you**;
   bind them around your neck,
   write them on the **tablet of your heart**.
⁴ Then you will **win favor** and a good name
   in the sight of God and man.
⁵ **Trust in the LORD** with all your heart
   and lean not on your own **understanding**;
⁶ in all your ways **submit** to him,
   and he will make your **paths straight**.

Discuss each of the highlighted words and phrases in this passage that guide us in the way of wisdom. Discuss how we can trust in the Lord daily.

Today's key verse: "Let love and faithfulness never leave you; bind them around your neck" (Proverbs 3:3).

Pray together: Lord, let love and faithfulness guide our lives today. May we trust in you with all of our hearts and lean on you, not our own understanding.

Weekly memory verse: "Trust in the LORD with all your heart and lean not on your own understanding; in all your ways submit to him, and he will make your paths straight" (Proverbs 3:5–6).

Shared Journal Experience: Turn to the Shared Journal Experience section for week 2, day 1, and share words of encouragement with each other.

SHARED JOURNAL EXPERIENCE

Week 2. Day 1

Mom

Share something fun you did when you were young that your son may not know! The key verse today (Proverbs 3:3) talks about love and faithfulness; is there a time when you felt surrounded by others who were loving and faithful?

_____

_____

_____

_____

_____

_____

_____

_____

_____

_____

_____

_____

_____

_____

_____

_____

_____

_____

_____

MEMORY VERSE

Trust in the LORD with all your heart
and lean not on your own understanding;

in all your ways submit to him,
and he will make your paths straight.

(Proverbs 3:5-6)

SHARED JOURNAL EXPERIENCE

Week 2. Day 1

Son

Is there something new you would like to learn? Share ideas with your mom and maybe suggest doing this together! How have you seen love and faithfulness in your home?

_____

_____

_____

_____

_____

_____

_____

_____

_____

_____

_____

_____

_____

_____

_____

_____

_____

_____

_____

TODAY'S KEY VERSE

Let love and faithfulness never leave you;
bind them around your neck.

(Proverbs 3:3)

WEEK 2

Day 2

Read and discuss Proverbs 3:7–12.

⁷ Do not **be wise in your own eyes;**
  fear the Lᴏʀᴅ and shun evil.
⁸ This will bring **health** to your body
  and nourishment to your bones.
⁹ **Honor the Lᴏʀᴅ** with your **wealth,**
  with the **firstfruits** of all your crops;
¹⁰ then your barns will be filled to overflowing,
  and your vats will brim over with new wine.
¹¹ My son, **do not despise the Lᴏʀᴅ's discipline,**
  and do not resent his **rebuke,**
¹² because **the Lᴏʀᴅ** disciplines those he loves,
  as a father the son he **delights** in.

Discuss each of the highlighted words and phrases that guide us in the ways of wisdom. Discuss how we can trust in the Lord daily.

Today's key verse: "Do not be wise in your own eyes; fear the Lᴏʀᴅ and shun evil" (Proverbs 3:7).

Pray together: Lord, may we not be wise in our own eyes and, instead, be quick to turn from evil and honour you in all we do.

Weekly memory verse: "Trust in the Lᴏʀᴅ with all your heart and lean not on your own understanding; in all your ways submit to him, and he will make your paths straight" (Proverbs 3:5–6).

Shared Journal Experience: Turn to the Shared Journal Experience section for week 2, day 2, and share words of encouragement with each other.

SHARED JOURNAL EXPERIENCE

Week 2, Day 2

Mom

Share a time when you trusted yourself instead of God. How did it turn out? Share a time when your son was trustworthy.

_____
_____
_____
_____
_____
_____
_____
_____
_____
_____
_____
_____
_____
_____
_____
_____
_____
_____
_____

MEMORY VERSE

*Trust in the LORD with all your heart
and lean not on your own understanding;*

*in all your ways submit to him,
and he will make your paths straight.*

(Proverbs 3:5-6)

SHARED JOURNAL EXPERIENCE

Week 2, Day 2

Son

How have you been trustworthy as a son, friend, or sibling? What does it mean to be responsible or faithful?

_____

_____

_____

_____

_____

_____

_____

_____

_____

_____

_____

_____

_____

_____

_____

_____

_____

_____

_____

_____

TODAY'S KEY VERSE

Do not be wise in your own eyes;
fear the LORD and shun evil.

(Proverbs 3:7)

WEEK 2

Day 3

Read and discuss Proverbs 3:13–18.

¹³ **Blessed** are those who find **wisdom**,
  those who **gain understanding,**
¹⁴ for she is **more profitable than silver**
  and **yields better returns than gold.**
¹⁵ **She is more precious than rubies**;
  nothing you desire can compare with her.
¹⁶ **Long life** is in her right hand;
  in her left hand are riches and honor.
¹⁷ Her ways are **pleasant ways,**
  and all her **paths are peace.**
¹⁸ She is a **tree of life** to those who take hold of her;
  those who hold her fast will **be blessed**.

Discuss each of the highlighted words and phrases in this passage that guide us in the ways of wisdom. Discuss how we can trust in the Lord daily.

Today's key verse: "Blessed are those who find wisdom, those who gain understanding" (Proverbs 3:13).

Pray together: Guide us, Lord, toward wisdom and understanding so our paths will be pleasant and peaceful.

Weekly memory verse: "Trust in the Lᴏʀᴅ with all your heart and lean not on your own understanding; in all your ways submit to him, and he will make your paths straight" (Proverbs 3:5–6).

Shared Journal Experience: Turn to the Shared Journal Experience section for week 2, day 3, and share words of encouragement with each other.

SHARED JOURNAL EXPERIENCE

Week 2. Day 3

Mom

Share paths of peace in your life and ways you have found understanding through God's Word.

_____

_____

_____

_____

_____

_____

_____

_____

_____

_____

_____

_____

_____

_____

_____

_____

_____

_____

MEMORY VERSE

*Trust in the LORD with all your heart
and lean not on your own understanding;*

*in all your ways submit to him,
and he will make your paths straight.*

(Proverbs 3:5-6)

SHARED JOURNAL EXPERIENCE

Week 2. Day 3

Son

How have you seen your mom act peacefully? How has she blessed you lately? Share a peaceful time you have experienced.

_____
_____
_____
_____
_____
_____
_____
_____
_____
_____
_____
_____
_____
_____
_____
_____
_____
_____
_____
_____
_____
_____

TODAY'S KEY VERSE

Blessed are those who find wisdom,
those who gain understanding.

(Proverbs 3:13)

WEEK 2

Day 4

Read together Proverbs 3:19–35.
Focus on and discuss Proverbs 19–27.

¹⁹ By **wisdom** the Lᴏʀᴅ laid the earth's foundations,
by **understanding he set the heavens in place**;
²⁰ by his **knowledge** the watery depths were divided,
and the clouds let drop the dew.
²¹ My son, **do not let wisdom and understanding out of your sight**,
preserve sound judgment and **discretion**;
²² they will be **life for you,**
an ornament to grace your neck.
²³ Then you will go on your way in **safety**,
and your foot will not stumble.
²⁴ When you lie down, **you will not be afraid**;
when you lie down, your **sleep will be sweet**.
²⁵ **Have no fear** of sudden disaster
or of the ruin that overtakes the wicked,
²⁶ for **the Lᴏʀᴅ** will be at your side
and will **keep your foot from being snared**.
²⁷ **Do not withhold good** from those to whom it is due,
when it is in your power to act.

Discuss each of the highlighted words and phrases in this passage that guide us in the way of wisdom. Discuss how we practically can trust in the Lord daily.

Today's key verse: "Do not withhold good from those to whom it is due, when it is in your power to act" (Proverbs 3:27).

Pray together: Lord, we ask for sound judgment and discretion so we can do good to others when it is in our power to act.

Weekly memory verse: "Trust in the Lᴏʀᴅ with all your heart and lean not on your own understanding; in all your ways submit to him, and he will make your paths straight" (Proverbs 3:5–6).

Shared Journal Experience: Turn to the Shared Journal Experience section for week 2, day 4, and share words of encouragement with each other.

SHARED JOURNAL EXPERIENCE

Week 2, Day 4

Mom

Share a time someone was good to you. Can you recall when you were able to do good to those for whom it was due when it was "in your power to act" (Proverbs 3:27)?

_____

_____

_____

_____

_____

_____

_____

_____

_____

_____

_____

_____

_____

_____

_____

_____

_____

MEMORY VERSE

*Trust in the LORD with all your heart
and lean not on your own understanding;*

*in all your ways submit to him,
and he will make your paths straight.*

(Proverbs 3:5–6)

SHARED JOURNAL EXPERIENCE

Week 2, Day 4

Son

Have you ever seen your mom do something good or helpful for others? What can you do for someone today that will be a blessing to them? Share some good things you see around your home.

_____

_____

_____

_____

_____

_____

_____

_____

_____

_____

_____

_____

_____

_____

_____

_____

_____

_____

_____

_____

_____

TODAY'S KEY VERSE

*Do not withhold good from those to whom it is due
when it is in your power to act.*

(Proverbs 3:27)

Day 5

Read together Proverbs 4:1–27.
Focus on and discuss Proverbs 4:10–18.

¹⁰ **Listen**, my son, **accept** what I say,
   and the **years of your life will be many**.
¹¹ I **instruct** you in **the way of wisdom**
   and **lead** you along **straight paths**.
¹² **When you walk**, your steps will **not be hampered**;
   when you run, you will **not stumble**.
¹³ **Hold** on to instruction, **do not let it go**;
   guard it well, for it is your life.
¹⁴ **Do not set foot on the path of the wicked**
   or walk in the way of evildoers.
¹⁵ **Avoid it**, do not travel on it;
   turn from it and go on your way.
¹⁶ For they **cannot rest** until they do evil;
   they are robbed of sleep till they **make someone stumble**.
¹⁷ They eat the bread of wickedness
   and drink the wine of violence.
¹⁸ The **path** of the **righteous** is like the **morning sun**,
   shining ever brighter till the full light of day.

Discuss each of the highlighted words and phrases in this passage that guide us in the way of wisdom. Discuss how we practically can trust in the Lord daily.

Today's key verse: "The path of the righteous is like the morning sun, shining ever brighter till the full light of day" (Proverbs 4:18).

Pray together: Lord, guide us on the shining path of the righteous and lead us away from the path of the wicked.

Weekly memory verse: "Trust in the LORD with all your heart and lean not on your own understanding; in all your ways submit to him, and he will make your paths straight" (Proverbs 3:5–6).

Shared Journal Experience: Turn to the Shared Journal Experience section for week 2, day 5, and share words of encouragement with each other.

SHARED JOURNAL EXPERIENCE

Week 2, Day 5

Mom

Share a time when a verse came to mind to help guide you on the path of life. What was the situation?

_____

_____

_____

_____

_____

_____

_____

_____

_____

_____

_____

_____

_____

_____

_____

_____

_____

_____

MEMORY VERSE

*Trust in the LORD with all your heart
and lean not on your own understanding;*

*in all your ways submit to him,
and he will make your paths straight.*

(Proverbs 3:5–6)

SHARED JOURNAL EXPERIENCE

Week 2. Day 5

Son

Share how your mom has helped guide you through a hard day.

_____
_____
_____
_____
_____
_____
_____
_____
_____
_____
_____
_____
_____
_____
_____
_____
_____
_____
_____
_____
_____
_____

TODAY'S KEY VERSE

*The path of the righteous is like the morning sun,
shining ever brighter till the full light of day.*

(Proverbs 4:18)

Day 5 – Ready, Set, Go

READY to be together

In Proverbs 4:18, we are reminded, "The path of the righteous is like the morning sun, shining ever brighter till the full light of day." Find time when you can set the alarm, rise early together, and watch the sunrise. Another option would be to observe the brilliance of the sun setting. Whatever you choose, make a date on the calendar to soak in the splendour of God's creation. Enjoy a time of silence, sharing moments of gratitude, praying together, simply chatting, or listening to worship music.

SET your music to worship

"Always Good" (Andrew Peterson)

"Christ is Risen" (Phil Wickham)

"How Good Is He" (Vertical Worship)

"Constellations" (Ellie Holcomb)

"God With Us" (We Are Messengers)

GO to read or listen to audiobooks or watch movies together

Listen or Watch

"The Pilgrims Progress" (Revelation Media)

"The Eric Liddell Story" (The Torchlighters: Heroes of the Faith)

"Charlie's Choice" (Lamplighter Ministries Dramatic Audio)

Read

Eric Liddell: Something Greater Than Gold (Janet and Geoff Benge)

Answers Books for Kids Box Set (Vol 1–8) (Ken Ham and Bodie Hodge)

Just for Mom

Women of the Word (Jen Wilkin)

The Right Kind of Strong (Mary Kassian)

Connector – Wisdom and Folly

Proverbs 5 and 6

Memory Verse

My son, pay attention to my wisdom;
turn your ear to my words of insight.
(Proverbs 5:1)

*How we view the world can lead toward a life-giving path
or destructive detour.*

Dear Mom,

Back in my youth, I looked forward to going to the local pop shop, a hidden treasure not far from our house. I couldn't see the storefront until the last second, but when I arrived, the door opened up to a world of flavour and colour. Knowing I would soon taste pink, orange, or grape soda made the experience deliciously dreamy. My eyes were fixed on the arrangement of glass bottles, row by row, waiting to be twisted and poured for my delight. I knew what I wanted before we entered the store; it was pink and bubbly. Inevitably, empty bottles appeared, and the bubbles stopped. Back I would go with my parents to return the empties in the well-known red plastic crate.

The hope for more always lingered. The thrill of the taste seemed to leave as quickly as it arrived. This is true of temptations in the world; they're within reach, gathered, consumed, and void of any nutritional value. I don't recall how often we went, but I do remember going with one or both of my parents. It's incredible how a last-minute thought a parent might have to include a child on an errand can be so impactful! The images of flavoured pop from years ago are reminders that temptation is always just around the corner. My eyes feasted on the variety of pop, but my parents determined how much and when and provided necessary guidance between my wants and needs.

It's easy to set our eyes on things in this world that promise instant satisfaction. We currently live in a culture that surrounds us like a gigantic theater with thunderous surround sound and is visually captivating. Turning off or tuning out the world can be an overwhelming challenge. What may be tempting to you will be entirely different for our sons. Including him in the conversation of what is hard to "turn off" or "tune out" for you allows him to see your weaknesses and, more importantly, your strengths in talking out loud about what may be a temptation.

These conversations are a gift to our sons and help keep us connected. Together, naming the various temptations leads us to solutions when we bring them before God in prayer. Leaving our unnamed temptations to linger in our minds allows them to fester and becomes a soundtrack in our heads on repeat. If we can say openly, "Son, I am tempted by...," he will likely be able to share what is enticing him.

Our heavenly Father longs for us to lean into his Word and gather wisdom so we can withstand the inevitable temptations that come our way.

> Be strong in the Lord and in his mighty power. Put on the full armor of God, so that you can take your stand against the devil's schemes. For our struggle is not against flesh and blood, but against the rulers, against the authorities, against the powers of this dark world and against the spiritual forces of evil in the heavenly realms. (Ephesians 6:10–12)

As we fall into step with God's Word daily, we prepare ourselves to guide our sons through timely words and remind them to be clothed in the fruit of the Spirit. "The fruit of the Spirit is love, joy, peace, patience, kindness, goodness, faithfulness, gentleness and self-control. Against such things there is no law" (Galatians 5:22–23). A Spirit-filled life allows us to take a stand against the schemes of the enemy and make wise, life-giving choices. Prayerfully we seek the Lord to guide our sons on a path of wisdom. And when temptation does come knocking, our sons will have biblical insights available to walk through the fire bravely, have faith, and remain rooted in Christ.

> This is what the LORD says—
> he who created you, Jacob,
> he who formed you, Israel:
> "Do not fear, for I have redeemed you;
> I have summoned you by name; you are mine.
> When you pass through the waters,
> I will be with you;
> and when you pass through the rivers,
> they will not sweep over you.
> When you walk through the fire,
> you will not be burned;
> the flames will not set you ablaze."
> (Isaiah 43:1–2)

WEEK 3

Day 1

Read together Proverbs 5:1–23.
Focus on and discuss Proverbs 5:1–6.

Warning Against Adultery

5 My son, **pay attention** to my **wisdom**,
   turn your ear to my words of **insight**,
² that you may **maintain discretion**
   and your lips may **preserve knowledge**.
³ For the lips of the adulterous woman drip honey,
   and **her speech** is smoother than oil;
⁴ but in the end she is **bitter** as gall,
   sharp as a double-edged sword.
⁵ Her feet go down to **death**;
   her steps lead **straight to the grave**.
⁶ She gives no thought to the **way of life**;
   her paths **wander aimlessly**, but **she does not know it**.

Discuss each of the highlighted words and phrases in this passage that provide warnings and guidance. How can we be more attentive to wisdom?

Today's key verse: "She gives no thought to the way of life; her paths wander aimlessly, but she does not know it" (Proverbs 5:6).

Pray together: Lord, lead us on the path of life so that we won't be tempted to wander aimlessly.

Weekly memory verse: "My son, pay attention to my wisdom; turn your ear to my words of insight" (Proverbs 5:1).

Shared Journal Experience: Turn to the Shared Journal Experience section for week 3, day 1, and share words of encouragement with each other.

SHARED JOURNAL EXPERIENCE

Week 3, Day 1

Mom

How have you been able to guard your heart, mind, and soul against the world's temptations?

_____

_____

_____

_____

_____

_____

_____

_____

_____

_____

_____

_____

_____

_____

_____

_____

_____

_____

MEMORY VERSE

My son, pay attention to my wisdom;
turn your ear to my words of insight.

(Proverbs 5:1)

SHARED JOURNAL EXPERIENCE

Week 3. Day 1

You

Have you ever been tempted to make unwise choices at home or school? Is there someone in your life you consider very wise? Share why you chose this person.

_____

_____

_____

_____

_____

_____

_____

_____

_____

_____

_____

_____

_____

_____

_____

_____

_____

_____

_____

_____

_____

TODAY'S KEY VERSE

She gives no thought to the way of life; her paths wander aimlessly, but she does not know it.

(Proverbs 5:6)

WEEK 3

Day 2

Read together Proverbs 6:1–11.
Focus on and discuss Proverbs 6:6–11.

6 Go to the ant, you **sluggard**;
   consider its **ways** and be **wise**!
7 It has no commander,
   no overseer or ruler,
8 yet it **stores its provisions** in summer
   and gathers its food at harvest.
9 **How long will you lie there**, you sluggard?
   When will you **get up from your sleep?**
10 A little **sleep**, a little **slumber**,
   a little **folding of the hands** to rest—
11 and **poverty** will come on you like a **thief**
   and scarcity like an armed man.

Discuss each of the highlighted words and phrases in this passage that provide warnings and guidance toward understanding. How can we be more attentive to wisdom?

Today's key verse: "Go to the ant, you sluggard; consider its ways and be wise!" (Proverbs 6:6).

Pray together: Lord, we ask for wisdom to guard against laziness and the temptation to act like a sluggard.

Weekly memory verse: "My son, pay attention to my wisdom; turn your ear to my words of insight" (Proverbs 5:1).

Shared Journal Experience: Turn to the Shared Journal Experience section for week 3, day 2, and share words of encouragement with each other.

SHARED JOURNAL EXPERIENCE

Week 3. Day 2

Mom

Share a time you did not accomplish all you had hoped. Then share a time when you successfully met your goals.

_____

_____

_____

_____

_____

_____

_____

_____

_____

_____

_____

_____

_____

_____

_____

_____

_____

_____

_____

_____

MEMORY VERSE

My son, pay attention to my wisdom;
turn your ear to my words of insight.

(Proverbs 5:1)

SHARED JOURNAL EXPERIENCE

Week 3. Day 2

Sons

Share a time you felt you worked as hard as the ant and accomplished something great. Have you ever been lazy like the sluggard described in Proverbs?

_____

_____

_____

_____

_____

_____

_____

_____

_____

_____

_____

_____

_____

_____

_____

_____

_____

_____

_____

_____

_____

TODAY'S KEY VERSE

Go to the ant, you sluggard;
consider its ways and be wise!

(Proverbs 6:6)

WEEK 3

Day 3

Read and discuss Proverbs 6:12–19.

¹² A **troublemaker** and a villain,
    who goes about with a **corrupt mouth**,
¹³ who winks **maliciously** with his eye,
    signals with his feet
    and **motions** with his fingers,
¹⁴ who **plots evil** with **deceit in his heart**—
    he always **stirs up conflict**.
¹⁵ Therefore **disaster** will overtake him in an **instant**;
    he will **suddenly** be destroyed—without remedy.
¹⁶ There are six things **the Lord** hates,
    seven that are **detestable** to him:
¹⁷ **haughty** eyes,
    a **lying** tongue,
    hands that shed **innocent** blood,
¹⁸ a **heart** that devises wicked **schemes**,
    feet that are quick to rush into evil,
¹⁹ a **false witness** who pours out lies
    and a person who **stirs up** conflict in the **community**.

Discuss each of the highlighted words and phrases in this passage that provide warnings and guidance toward understanding. How can we be more attentive to wisdom?

Today's key verse: "Disaster will overtake him in an instant; he will suddenly be destroyed—without remedy" (Proverbs 6:15).

Pray together: Lord, show us ways to be a blessing to others and have a heart of service.

Weekly memory verse: "My son, pay attention to my wisdom; turn your ear to my words of insight" (Proverbs 5:1).

Shared Journal Experience: Turn to the Shared Journal Experience section for week 3, day 3, and share words of encouragement with each other.

SHARED JOURNAL EXPERIENCE

Week 3, Day 3

Mom

Have you experienced a trial in a community setting? Share a blessing that you experienced from that same community.

_____

_____

_____

_____

_____

_____

_____

_____

_____

_____

_____

_____

_____

_____

_____

_____

_____

_____

_____

MEMORY VERSE

My son, pay attention to my wisdom;
turn your ear to my words of insight.

(Proverbs 5:1)

SHARED JOURNAL EXPERIENCE

Week 3. Day 3

Son

Share how a friend or family member has made you feel special and loved. How can you creatively show care to someone else, such as a neighbour, friend from church, or someone in your own home?

_____

_____

_____

_____

_____

_____

_____

_____

_____

_____

_____

_____

_____

_____

_____

_____

_____

_____

TODAY'S KEY VERSE

Disaster will overtake him in an instant;
he will suddenly be destroyed — without remedy.

(Proverbs 6:15)

Read and discuss Proverbs 6:20–26.

Warning Against Adultery

²⁰ My son, **keep your Father's command**
and do not **forsake your mother's teaching.**
²¹ **Bind** them always on **your heart**;
fasten them around your neck.
²² **When you walk**, they will guide you;
when you sleep, they will watch over you;
when you awake, they will speak to you.
²³ For this **command** is a **lamp**,
this **teaching** is a **light**,
and **correction** and **instruction**
are the way to **life**,
²⁴ **keeping** you from your neighbor's wife,
from the **smooth talk** of a wayward woman.
²⁵ Do not **lust in your heart** after her beauty
or let her **captivate** you with her eyes.
²⁶ For a prostitute can be had for a loaf of bread,
but another man's wife preys on **your very life.**

Discuss each of the highlighted words and phrases in this passage that provide warnings and guidance toward understanding. How can we be more attentive to wisdom?

Today's key verse: "My son, keep your father's command and do not forsake your mother's teaching. Bind them always on your heart; fasten them around your neck" (Proverbs 6:20–21).

Pray together: Lord, captivate our hearts with your unfailing love while we walk, when we sleep, and when we are awake. May we keep your commands always in our hearts.

Weekly memory verse: "My son, pay attention to my wisdom; turn your ear to my words of insight" (Proverbs 5:1).

Shared Journal Experience: Turn to the Shared Journal Experience section for week 3, day 4, and share words of encouragement with each other.

SHARED JOURNAL EXPERIENCE

Week 3. Day 4

Mom

Can you recall when someone shared wisdom with you and helped guide you through a specific trial or temptation? Share what you learned.

_____

_____

_____

_____

_____

_____

_____

_____

_____

_____

_____

_____

_____

_____

_____

_____

_____

_____

_____

_____

MEMORY VERSE

My son, pay attention to my wisdom;
turn your ear to my words of insight.

(Proverbs 5:1)

SHARED JOURNAL EXPERIENCE

Week 3. Day 4

Son

How have you been tempted to let something captivate or take hold of your heart? Share how your family has helped you overcome the temptation. How would you help a friend or family member make a wise choice?

_____

_____

_____

_____

_____

_____

_____

_____

_____

_____

_____

_____

_____

_____

_____

_____

_____

TODAY'S KEY VERSE

*My son, keep your father's command
and do not forsake your mother's teaching.*

*Bind them always on your heart;
fasten them around your neck.*

(Proverbs 6:20-21)

WEEK 3

Day 5

Read and discuss Proverbs 6:27–35.

27 Can a man scoop **fire** into his lap
   without his clothes being **burned**?
28 Can a man **walk** on hot coals
   without his feet being scorched?
29 So is he who sleeps with another man's wife;
   no one who touches her will go **unpunished**.
30 People do not **despise** a thief if he steals
   to **satisfy** his hunger when he is starving.
31 Yet if he is **caught**, he must pay sevenfold,
   though it costs him all the wealth of his house.
32 But a man who **commits** adultery has **no sense**;
   whoever does so **destroys himself**.
33 Blows and **disgrace** are **his lot,**
   and his **shame** will never be wiped away.
34 For **jealousy** arouses a husband's fury,
   and he will show no mercy when he takes **revenge**.
35 He will not accept any compensation;
   he will refuse a bribe, however great it is.

Discuss each of the highlighted words and phrases in this passage that provide warnings and guidance toward understanding. How can we be more attentive to wisdom?

Today's key verse: "Can a man scoop fire into his lap without his clothes being burned?" (Proverbs 6:27).

Pray together: May we, Lord, be wise and attentive to temptations that come our way.

Weekly memory verse: "My son, pay attention to my wisdom; turn your ear to my words of insight" (Proverbs 5:1).

Shared Journal Experience: Turn to the Shared Journal Experience section for week 3, day 5, and share words of encouragement with each other.

SHARED JOURNAL EXPERIENCE

Week 3. Day 5

Mom

Proverbs tackles challenging issues of fidelity and commitment with striking language that hits hard, like "no mercy" and "revenge". Share with your son today your thoughts on commitment in relationships. Perhaps there is a time when someone demonstrated mercy, grace, and wholeness to you. Maybe there is a time you felt betrayed, and you can share how you navigated that challenge. Remind your son today we are all sinners in need of grace (Ephesians 2:8), we are all made in the image of God (Genesis 1:27), and when we ask forgiveness of our sins, they are removed from us (Psalm 103:12). We are never too far gone from the love of Jesus!

_____
_____
_____
_____
_____
_____
_____
_____
_____
_____
_____
_____
_____
_____

MEMORY VERSE

My son, pay attention to my wisdom;
turn your ear to my words of insight.

(Proverbs 5:1)

SHARED JOURNAL EXPERIENCE

Week 3. Day 5

Son

Have you had to show forgiveness to someone? If so, how did you feel after forgiving them? What is it like to ask forgiveness from others?

_____

_____

_____

_____

_____

_____

_____

_____

_____

_____

_____

_____

_____

_____

_____

_____

_____

_____

_____

TODAY'S KEY VERSE

Can a man scoop fire into his lap
without his clothes being burned?

(Proverbs 6:27)

Day 5 – Ready, Set, Go

READY to be together

According to Proverbs 6:6, ants are hard workers! Today research how ant colonies work so succinctly. Maybe look into owning a small ant farm, or you may prefer to watch the ants bustling in your yard. Whatever you decide, it is incredible to observe their uniquely created design and purpose. Remind each other that we are made in the image of God with a purpose and plan beyond what we can imagine (Ephesians 3:20).

SET your music to worship

"Sweet Jesus" (Crowder & Maverick City)

"Mention of Your Name" (Jenn Johnson)

"Image of God" (Acoustic, We Are Messengers and Vince Gill)

"Act Justly, Love Mercy, Walk Humbly" (Par Barrett)

"Joseph A Song of Surrender" (Cliff Cline)

GO to read or listen to audiobooks or watch movies together

Listen or Watch

"Charlie's Choice, The Wanderer" (Lamplighter Ministries Dramatic Audio)

"Courageous" (Kendrick Brothers)

Read

Seven Women and the Secret of Their Greatness (Eric Metaxas)

Seven Men and the Secret of Their Greatness (Eric Metaxas)

Just for Mom

Devoted (Tim Challies)

Holier Than Thou (Jackie Hill Perry)

Provider – The Way of Wisdom

Memory Verse

Now then, my children, listen to me;
blessed are those who keep my ways.
Listen to my instruction and be wise;
do not disregard it.
(Proverbs 8:32–33)

Wisdom from God's Word leaves us feeling assured,
filled with truth, and awestruck.

Dear Mom,

I have precious memories of extended family gathered for picnic lunches beside a slow-moving river lined with towering willow trees. It provided the perfect scenery for adventure and more memory-making. The cousins would float together on large black tubes down the murky river hoping to be out of the way of the crazy ones swinging from branches or soaring from a ramp on their bikes into the water! I am sure the parents had a watchful eye on the kids while tubes flipped or prepared to rescue us when we floated just a little too far!

All of us have gone off course at some point in our lives. We have fallen into cloudy waters and felt like we are sinking. But, the good news is that we are never too far gone down rapids for the Lord to lovingly guide us to safety. Luke 12:6–7 is a timely reminder of God's love, "Are not five sparrows sold for two pennies? Yet not one of them is forgotten by God. Indeed, the very hairs of your head are all numbered. Don't be afraid; you are worth more than many sparrows." He created us, he knows us, and he loves us dearly.

Sometimes, the wisdom we seek to share with our sons is not received as we hope. They may choose to take a lazy, winding river and end up sun-scorched, hungry, and unsure which turn to take. Our sons may take a path we never intended or hoped for, but the Lord has placed us in their lives on purpose to be a provider of wisdom and grace.

As moms, we serve and show love in multifaceted ways. We love because Christ loved us first (1 John 4:19); we serve because Christ came to serve (Matthew 20:28). Each time we do, we steadfastly pray they receive and take hold of what we share with them in their lives. We trust the Holy Spirit to soften and prepare their hearts for whatever God is calling them to do. The foundation we provide by opening the Word of God and praying with and for our sons while cultivating the beautiful blessing of community is the gift we give.

You are not alone on this parenting journey, "So do not fear, for I am with you; do not be dismayed, for I am your God. I will strengthen you and help you; I will uphold you with my righteous right hand" (Isaiah 41:10). There are days when fear consumes, doubt creeps in, and lies linger, tempting us to question if we can be the mom we hope to be for our son. Be encouraged, we do not need to parent on our own strength! We have a perfect God who goes before us. We need to commit to him our fears and believe that he is a God that sees and knows our needs (Genesis 16:13).

I love the reminder in Deuteronomy to make this a way of life in our homes.

"Hear, O Israel: The LORD our God, the LORD is one. Love the LORD your God with all your heart and with all your soul and with all your strength. These commandments that I give you today are to be on your hearts. Impress them on your children. Talk about them when you sit at home and when you walk along the road, when you lie down and when you get up. Tie them as symbols on your hands and bind them on your foreheads. Write them on the doorframes of your houses and on your gates." (6:4–9)

Day 1

Read together Proverbs 7:1–15.
Focus on and discuss Proverbs 7:1–9.

Warning Against the Adulterous Woman

7 My son, **keep my words**
    and **store up my commands** within you.
² Keep my commands and **you will live;**
    guard my teachings as the apple of your eye.
³ **Bind them** on your fingers;
    write them on the tablet of **your heart**.
⁴ Say to **wisdom**, "You are my sister,"
    and to **insight**, "You are my relative."
⁵ **They will keep you** from the adulterous woman,
    from the **wayward** woman with her seductive words.
⁶ At the window of my house
    I looked down through the lattice.
⁷ I saw among the **simple**,
    I noticed among the young men,
    a youth who had no sense.
⁸ He was going down the street near her corner,
    walking along in the **direction** of her house
⁹ at twilight, as the day was fading,
    as the **dark of night** set in.

Discuss each of the highlighted words and phrases in this passage that provide insight into living life walking in wisdom. How can we hold fast to God's commandments and treasure them in our hearts?

Today's key verse: "Keep my commands and you will live; guard my teachings as the apple of your eye" (Proverbs 7:2).

Pray together: Lord, graciously lead us toward your teaching, and keep us on the path of wisdom and insight.

Weekly memory verse: "Now then, my children, listen to me; blessed are those who keep my ways. Listen to my instruction and be wise; do not disregard it" (Proverbs 8:32–33).

Shared Journal Experience: Turn to the Shared Journal Experience section for week 4, day 1, and share words of encouragement with each other.

SHARED JOURNAL EXPERIENCE

Week 4, Day 1

Mom

Share what accountability means to you and how you can act this out together. If this is a new concept, introduce it today and discuss the benefits of accountability for you personally.

_____

_____

_____

_____

_____

_____

_____

_____

_____

_____

_____

_____

_____

_____

_____

_____

_____

MEMORY VERSE

Now then, my children, listen to me;
blessed are those who keep my ways.

Listen to my instruction and be wise;
do not disregard it.

(Proverbs 8:32–33)

SHARED JOURNAL EXPERIENCE

Week 4. Day 1

Son

Have you ever had to guard something that was special to you? How did it feel to protect this item? Share how you can protect your heart from unwise choices.

_____
_____
_____
_____
_____
_____
_____
_____
_____
_____
_____
_____
_____
_____
_____
_____
_____
_____
_____
_____
_____

TODAY'S KEY VERSE

Keep my commands and you will live;
guard my teachings as the apple of your eye.

(Proverbs 7:2)

WEEK 4

Day 2

Read together Proverbs 7:16–27.
Focus on and discuss Proverbs 7:24–27.

²⁴ Now then, **my sons**, **listen to me**;
pay attention to what I say.
²⁵ **Do not let your heart turn** to her ways
or **stray** into her paths.
²⁶ Many are the victims she has **brought down**;
her slain are a mighty throng.
²⁷ Her house is a **highway to the grave**,
leading down to the chambers of death.

Discuss each of the highlighted words and phrases in this passage that provide insight into living life walking in wisdom. How can we hold fast to God's commandments and treasure them in our hearts?

Today's key verse: "Now then, my sons, listen to me; pay attention to what I say" (Proverbs 7:25).

Pray together: Lord, may we have the ability to pay attention to your Word and keep our hearts from turning from your ways.

Weekly memory verse: "Now then, my children, listen to me; blessed are those who keep my ways. Listen to my instruction and be wise; do not disregard it" (Proverbs 8.32–33).

Shared Journal Experience: Turn to the Shared Journal Experience section for week 4, day 2, and share words of encouragement with each other.

SHARED JOURNAL EXPERIENCE

Week 4. Day 2
Mom

Today remind your son of a time he listened to your teaching. How was he blessed because of this choice?

_____

_____

_____

_____

_____

_____

_____

_____

_____

_____

_____

_____

_____

_____

_____

_____

_____

_____

MEMORY VERSE

Now then, my children, listen to me;
blessed are those who keep my ways.

Listen to my instruction and be wise;
do not disregard it.

(Proverbs 8:32–33)

SHARED JOURNAL EXPERIENCE

Week 4. Day 2

Son

Today write out words of blessing to each person in your family. Can you think of ways to bless your family today secretly?

_____

_____

_____

_____

_____

_____

_____

_____

_____

_____

_____

_____

_____

_____

_____

_____

_____

_____

_____

_____

_____

_____

TODAY'S KEY VERSE

Now then, my sons, listen to me;
pay attention to what I say.

(Proverbs 7:25)

Day 3

Read and discuss Proverbs 8:1–11.

Wisdom's Call

8 Does not **wisdom call out**?
  Does not understanding **raise her voice**?
² At the highest point along the way,
  where the paths meet, she **takes her stand**;
³ beside the gate leading into the city,
  at the entrance, **she cries aloud**:
⁴ "To you, O people, **I call out**;
  I raise my voice to all mankind.
⁵ You who are **simple**, gain prudence;
  you who are foolish, set your hearts on it.
⁶ Listen, for I have **trustworthy things to say**;
  I open my lips to **speak what is right**.
⁷ My mouth speaks **what is true**,
  for **my lips detest wickedness**.
⁸ All the **words** of my mouth are **just**;
  none of them is crooked or perverse.
⁹ To the **discerning** all of them are **right**;
  they are **upright** to those who have found knowledge.
¹⁰ **Choose my instruction** instead of silver,
  knowledge rather than choice gold,
¹¹ for **wisdom is more precious than rubies**,
  and nothing you desire can compare with her."

Discuss each of the highlighted words and phrases in this passage that provide insight into living life walking in wisdom. How can we hold fast to God's commandments and treasure them in our hearts?

Today's key verse: "Choose my instruction instead of silver, knowledge rather than choice gold, for wisdom is more precious than rubies, and nothing you desire can compare with her" (Proverbs 8:10–11).

Pray together: Lord, guide us in your trustworthy ways, and help us to set our hearts on your wisdom and speak what is right and true.

Weekly memory verse: "Now then, my children, listen to me; blessed are those who keep my ways. Listen to my instruction and be wise; do not disregard it" (Proverbs 8:32–33).

Shared Journal Experience: Turn to the Shared Journal Experience section for week 4, day 3, and share words of encouragement with each other.

SHARED JOURNAL EXPERIENCE

Week 4. Day 3

Mom

How has wisdom "called out" (Proverbs 8:1) in your life?

_____

_____

_____

_____

_____

_____

_____

_____

_____

_____

_____

_____

_____

_____

_____

_____

_____

_____

_____

_____

MEMORY VERSE

Now then, my children, listen to me;
blessed are those who keep my ways.

Listen to my instruction and be wise;
do not disregard it.

(Proverbs 8:32–33)

SHARED JOURNAL EXPERIENCE

Week 4, Day 3

Son

Proverbs 8:6 says, "Listen, for I have trustworthy things to say; I open my lips to speak what is right." What does it mean to speak what is right?

_____

_____

_____

_____

_____

_____

_____

_____

_____

_____

_____

_____

_____

_____

_____

_____

_____

_____

TODAY'S KEY VERSE

Choose my instruction instead of silver,
knowledge rather than choice gold,

for wisdom is more precious than rubies,
and nothing you desire can compare with her.

(Proverbs 8:10-11)

WEEK 4

Day 4

Read together Proverbs 8:12–21.
Focus on and discuss 8:12–17.

¹² I, wisdom, **dwell together** with prudence;
    I possess **knowledge and discretion**.
¹³ To **fear the Lord** is to hate evil;
    I hate **pride and arrogance**,
    evil behavior and perverse speech.
¹⁴ Counsel and **sound judgment** are mine;
    I have **insight**, I have **power**.
¹⁵ By me kings reign
    and rulers issue decrees that are just;
¹⁶ by me princes govern,
    and nobles—all who rule on earth.
¹⁷ **I love those who love me**,
    and those who **seek me** find me.

Discuss each of the highlighted words and phrases in this passage that provide insight into living life walking in wisdom. How can we hold fast to God's commandments and treasure them in our hearts?

Today's key verse: "I love those who love me, and those who seek me find me" (Proverbs 8:17).

Pray together: Lord, we ask that you provide us with sound judgment, insight, knowledge, and discretion.

Weekly memory verse: "Now then, my children, listen to me; blessed are those who keep my ways. Listen to my instruction and be wise; do not disregard it" (Proverbs 8:32–33).

Shared Journal Experience: Turn to the Shared Journal Experience section for week 4, day 4, and share words of encouragement with each other.

SHARED JOURNAL EXPERIENCE

Week 4. Day 4

Mom

Share with your son a time you had sound judgment and a time you feel you did not and what unfolded.

_____

_____

_____

_____

_____

_____

_____

_____

_____

_____

_____

_____

_____

_____

_____

_____

_____

_____

_____

MEMORY VERSE

Now then, my children, listen to me;
blessed are those who keep my ways.

Listen to my instruction and be wise;
do not disregard it.

(Proverbs 8:32–33)

SHARED JOURNAL EXPERIENCE

Week 4. Day 4

Son

Do you have a favourite hero, perhaps someone from the Bible, a character from a movie or book series? Maybe you know your hero personally. What makes them special?

_____

_____

_____

_____

_____

_____

_____

_____

_____

_____

_____

_____

_____

_____

_____

_____

_____

_____

_____

_____

TODAY'S KEY VERSE

I love those who love me,
and those who seek me find me.

(Proverbs 8:17)

WEEK 4

Day 5

Read together Proverbs 8:22–36.
Focus on and discuss Proverbs 8:32–36.

³² Now then, my children, **listen to me**;
    blessed are those who keep my ways.
³³ Listen to my **instruction** and **be wise**;
    do not disregard it.
³⁴ **Blessed** are those who listen to me,
    watching daily at my doors,
    waiting at my doorway.
³⁵ For those who find me **find life**
    and receive **favor from the Lord**.
³⁶ But those who **fail** to find me harm themselves;
    all who hate me **love death**.

Discuss each of the highlighted words and phrases in this passage that provide insight into living life walking in wisdom. How can we hold fast to God's commandments and treasure them in our hearts?

Today's key verse: "Blessed are those who listen to me, watching daily at my doors, waiting at my doorway" (Proverbs 8:34).

Pray together: Lord, help us listen to God's instruction, act wisely, and treasure your wisdom in our hearts.

Weekly memory verse: "Now then, my children, listen to me; blessed are those who keep my ways. Listen to my instruction and be wise; do not disregard it" (Proverbs 8:32–33).

Shared Journal Experience: Turn to the Shared Journal Experience section for week 4, day 5, and share words of encouragement with each other.

SHARED JOURNAL EXPERIENCE

Week 4. Day 5

Mom

Share a memory today from when you were young that makes you laugh! How does your son bring joy to your home?

_____
_____
_____
_____
_____
_____
_____
_____
_____
_____
_____
_____
_____
_____
_____
_____
_____
_____

MEMORY VERSE

Now then, my children, listen to me;
blessed are those who keep my ways.

Listen to my instruction and be wise;
do not disregard it.

(Proverbs 8:32–33)

SHARED JOURNAL EXPERIENCE

Week 4. Day 5

Son

Create a plan today to creatively bless your mom. Write down ways she blesses you!

_____
_____
_____
_____
_____
_____
_____
_____
_____
_____
_____
_____
_____
_____
_____
_____
_____
_____
_____
_____
_____
_____

TODAY'S KEY VERSE

Blessed are those who listen to me,
watching daily at my doors,
waiting at my doorway.

(Proverbs 8:34)

Take Action!

Day 5 – Ready, Set, Go

READY to be together

This is a "pack up and go" kind of day. Plan for an outing that includes a lunch-to-go and hiking trails. Perhaps you can choose to go to a local conservation area where you can enjoy time alone, and bring along an easy-to-pack game. Don't forget to take pictures!

SET your music to worship

"Perfectly Loved" (Rachael Lampa featuring TobyMac)

"High Up" (Jonathon Traylor)

"Note To Self" (Stephen Stanley and Riley Clemmons)

"My Jesus" (Anne Wilson featuring Crowder)

"Thank You, Lord" (Chris Tomlin featuring Thomas Rhett and Florida Georgia Line)

GO to read or listen to audiobooks or watch movies together

Listen

"The Lion, Witch and the Wardrobe" (Focus on the Family Audio Resource)

"The Jim Elliot Story" (Torchlighters Heroes of the Faith)

Read

How Great Is Our God – 100 Indescribable Devotions About God and Science (Louie Giglio)

Brave Heroes and Bold Defenders 50 True Stories of Daring Men of God (Shirley Raye Redmond)

Just for Mom

In His Image (Jen Wilkin)

New Morning Mercies (Paul David Tripp)

Listener – Apply and Build

Proverbs 9 and 10

Memory Verse
Wisdom has built her house;
she has set up its seven pillars.
(Proverbs 9:1)

*Creating memories for our children is a layering of wise words and actions
so they can one day impart them to their children.*

Dear Mom,

I witnessed my parents envision a backyard paradise for their four kids. It was pieced together in front of us like a puzzle. The lumber and supplies turned into a treehouse complete with a wooden staircase, swings, spinning tire, and mini zip line. It wasn't tree trekking and soaring over the lush forests of Costa Rica, but the thrill of holding on for dear life while zipping down the line and hitting the spare tires at the end was all we needed. Way ahead of his time in creativity, my dad constructed a playground well known to all the neighbourhood kids in our tiny backyard (that was massive in our eyes). My mom, a gracious hostess, opened our front door, side gate, and fridge for our neighbourhood friends.

Our garden was humble, but we were each given a small square to plant a few items. I only recall sunflowers. The above-ground pool stood maybe three feet tall, just enough to cool us down and for all four kids to run in circles to create a whirlpool. Then we would turn abruptly to go against the current as though on a rescue mission. Enter the orange rectangular trampoline. We spent countless hours jumping, sleeping under the stars, and wildly adding water and dish soap on hot summer days. Our backyard required commitment from my parents to create this mini paradise. They listened well to our needs, and it kept us happily occupied!

As we navigate Proverbs, the theme of wisdom calling to us continues. Are we listening to the tender yet persistent call of Lady Wisdom in our lives? Our sons will hear different voices and forms of worldly wisdom that can lead them toward building a faulty life structure and may require a complete makeover.

Remember, we all need to be made new: "If anyone is in Christ, the new creation has come: The old has gone, the new is here!" (2 Corinthians 5:17). We bring our sons to the feet of Jesus. He is the heart-changer! We can read the Word, point them to Scripture, and pray consistently that the truth nestles into both the short- and long-term storehouses of their minds, and by God's grace, it will. The rest is up to an almighty, sovereign, and loving God.

We might pray fervently for our sons to follow Jesus—a prayer which may go unanswered for many years. When we are tempted to lose hope or be overcome with sadness, where are we looking for assurance? Jesus's disciples felt sorrow in their hearts too. Jesus shared before his betrayal and death, "You are filled with grief because I have said these things" (John 16:6). Jesus continues, "Very truly I tell you, it is for your good that I am going away. Unless I go away, the Advocate will not come to you; but if I go, I will send him to you" (John 16:7). The gift of the Holy Spirit has been given to comfort and lead us; "When he, the Spirit of truth, comes, he will guide you into all the truth. He will not speak on his own; he will speak only what he hears, and he will tell you what is yet to come" (John 16:13) We have an advocate! (John 15:26). What a wonderful promise this is for us to believe—we are not alone. When there is a temptation to lose heart and question if you are worthy of the calling to be a mom, listen to the words Jesus shares: "I have told you these things, so that in me you may have peace. In this world you will have trouble. But take heart! I have overcome the world" (John 16:33). God has called us and will equip us for the task; nothing is impossible for God.

Even as we share God's Word with our sons, and attempt to live it out daily, we, too, can miss the voice of wisdom and follow our desires. These moments are worthy of sharing with our sons so they understand we are all God's children in need of correction, "All Scripture is God-breathed and is useful for teaching, rebuking, correcting and training in righteousness, so that the servant of God may be thoroughly equipped for every good work" (2 Timothy 3:16–17). We have been given the wonderful opportunity to listen to our sons' needs while pointing them to God's Word, allowing them to see how God works graciously in our lives.

Proverbs is full of wise words, corrections, warnings, and what is right and true and helpful for gaining insight into our daily lives. It is worth every effort to encourage our sons with the habit of reading these wise sayings and acting on what we have read. Our need for wisdom from the book of Proverbs is a constant reminder to keep our eyes fixed on Jesus. The Bible is the ultimate blueprint for constructing a life full of wisdom.

My parents listened to the needs of their children and pursued a vision for our backyard playground that would provide hours of creative play. It required planning and implementation. We, too, need to make plans to seek the wisdom we read in Proverbs and allow it to frame our hearts and homes and leave the salvation of our sons in his hands.

WEEK 5

Day 1

Read and discuss Proverbs 9:1–6.

Invitations of Wisdom and Folly

9 **Wisdom has built her house;**
    she has **set up** its seven pillars.
² She has **prepared** her meat and mixed her wine;
    she has also **set** her table.
³ She has sent out her servants, and **she calls**
    from the highest point of the city,
⁴ "Let all who are simple **come to my house!**"
To those who have **no sense** she says,
⁵ "Come, eat my food
    and drink the wine I have mixed.
⁶ **Leave your simple ways** and **you will live;**
    walk in the way of insight."

Discuss each of the highlighted words and phrases in this passage that lead us toward building a solid foundation in Christ. How can you walk in the way of insight today?

Today's key verse: "Leave your simple ways and you will live; walk in the way of insight" (Proverbs 9:6).

Pray together: Lord, show us how to walk in the way of wisdom and build our house on insight.

Weekly memory verse: "Wisdom has built her house; she has set up its seven pillars" (Proverbs 9:1).

Shared Journal Experience: Turn to the Shared Journal Experience section for week 5, day 1, and share words of encouragement with each other.

SHARED JOURNAL EXPERIENCE

Week 5. Day 1

Mom

Who has influenced you the most in your life? How has your son inspired you? Plan a special time out together—your choice. Surprise him!

_____

_____

_____

_____

_____

_____

_____

_____

_____

_____

_____

_____

_____

_____

_____

_____

_____

_____

MEMORY VERSE

Wisdom has built her house;
she has set up its seven pillars.

(Proverbs 9:1)

SHARED JOURNAL EXPERIENCE

Week 5. Day 1

Son

Today, write a note, design a picture, or use another creative way to share a wise word or a verse for someone in your family from Proverbs. Share with your mom why you chose this wise word or verse.

_____

_____

_____

_____

_____

_____

_____

_____

_____

_____

_____

_____

_____

_____

_____

_____

_____

_____

_____

TODAY'S KEY VERSE

Leave your simple ways and you will live;
walk in the way of insight.

(Proverbs 9:6)

Day 2

Read and discuss Proverbs 9:7–12.

7 Whoever **corrects** a mocker **invites insults;**
   whoever rebukes the wicked incurs abuse.
8 Do not rebuke mockers or they will hate you;
   rebuke the wise and they will **love** you.
9 Instruct the **wise** and they will be **wiser still;**
   teach the righteous and they will **add to their learning**.
10 The **fear of the Lord** is the **beginning of wisdom,**
   and **knowledge** of **the Holy One** is **understanding**.
11 For through **wisdom your days will be many,**
   and years will be added to your life.
12 If you are wise, your **wisdom will reward you;**
   if you are a **mocker**, you alone will suffer.

Discuss each of the highlighted words and phrases in this passage that lead us toward building a solid foundation in Christ. How can you walk in the way of insight today?

Today's key verse: "Instruct the wise and they will be wiser still; teach the righteous and they will add to their learning" (Proverbs 9:9).

Pray together: Guide us, Lord, as we receive wise instruction and teaching from your Word so we can gain knowledge and understanding and apply it to our lives.

Weekly memory verse: "Wisdom has built her house; she has set up its seven pillars" (Proverbs 9:1).

Shared Journal Experience: Turn to the Shared Journal Experience section for week 5, day 2, and share words of encouragement with each other.

SHARED JOURNAL EXPERIENCE

Week 5. Day 2
Mom

Proverbs 9:1 says, "Wisdom has built her house; she has set up its seven pillars." How does your son "build up" your home with wisdom?

_____

_____

_____

_____

_____

_____

_____

_____

_____

_____

_____

_____

_____

_____

_____

_____

_____

_____

_____

_____

_____

_____

MEMORY VERSE

Wisdom has built her house;
she has set up its seven pillars.

(Proverbs 9:1)

SHARED JOURNAL EXPERIENCE

Week 5. Day 2

Son

Share a time when you began a new project and learned something new. How did it feel to complete this with others or on your own? Is there something new you would like to try with your mom?

_____

_____

_____

_____

_____

_____

_____

_____

_____

_____

_____

_____

_____

_____

_____

_____

_____

_____

_____

TODAY'S KEY VERSE

*Instruct the wise and they will be wiser still;
teach the righteous and they will add to their learning.*

(Proverbs 9:9)

Day 3

Read and discuss Proverbs 9:13–18.

¹³ Folly is an **unruly** woman;
　　she is **simple** and knows nothing.
¹⁴ She sits at the door of her house,
　　on a seat at the **highest point** of the city,
¹⁵ calling out to those who pass by,
　　who go straight on their way,
¹⁶ "**Let all who are simple** come to my house!"
To those who have **no sense** she says,
¹⁷ "**Stolen** water is sweet;
　　food eaten in **secret** is delicious!"
¹⁸ **But little do they know** that the dead are there,
　　that her guests are **deep in the realm of the dead**.

Discuss each of the highlighted words and phrases in this passage that lead us toward building a solid foundation in Christ. How can you walk in the way of insight today? How can you guard yourself against foolishness?

Today's key verse: "'Let all who are simple come to my house!' To those who have no sense she says, 'Stolen water is sweet; food eaten in secret is delicious!'" (Proverbs 9:16–17).

Pray together: Lord, guide us every day to listen to your voice and have the sense to know the difference between wisdom and foolishness.

Weekly memory verse: "Wisdom has built her house; she has set up its seven pillars" (Proverbs 9:1).

Shared Journal Experience: Turn to the Shared Journal Experience section for week 5, day 3, and share words of encouragement with each other.

SHARED JOURNAL EXPERIENCE

Week 5. Day 3

Mom

Today, share how your son can stand guard against the enemy's schemes based on Ephesians 6:10–20 and Matthew 7:15. Read these verses out loud together.

_____
_____
_____
_____
_____
_____
_____
_____
_____
_____
_____
_____
_____
_____
_____
_____
_____
_____
_____
_____
_____
_____

MEMORY VERSE

Wisdom has built her house;
she has set up its seven pillars.

(Proverbs 9:1)

SHARED JOURNAL EXPERIENCE

Week 5, Day 3

Son

After listening to your mom read Ephesians 6:10–20, what armour of God stands out to you, and why? (The armour of God includes the belt of truth, the breastplate of righteousness, sandals of peace, the shield of faith, the helmet of salvation, and the sword of the Spirit.)

_____

_____

_____

_____

_____

_____

_____

_____

_____

_____

_____

_____

_____

_____

_____

_____

_____

TODAY'S KEY VERSE

"Let all who are simple come to my house!"

To those who have no sense she says,
"Stolen water is sweet;
food eaten in secret is delicious!"

(Proverbs 9:16–17)

WEEK 5

Day 4

Read together Proverbs 10:1–16.
Focus on and discuss Proverbs 10:1–8.

10 The proverbs of Solomon:
A wise son brings joy to his father,
    but **a foolish son brings grief** to his mother.
² Ill-gotten treasures have no lasting value,
    but **righteousness delivers** from death.
³ The LORD does not let the **righteous** go hungry,
    but he **thwarts** the craving of the wicked.
⁴ **Lazy hands** make for poverty,
    but **diligent hands** bring wealth.
⁵ He who **gathers** crops in summer is a **prudent son**,
    but he who sleeps during harvest is a **disgraceful son**.
⁶ Blessings crown the head of the righteous,
    but **violence overwhelms** the mouth of the wicked.
⁷ The name of the righteous is used in blessings,
    but the name of the **wicked** will rot.
⁸ The wise in heart accept commands,
    but a **chattering fool** comes to ruin.

Discuss each of the highlighted words and phrases in this passage that lead us toward building a solid foundation in Christ. How can you walk in the way of insight today? How can your words and actions be a blessing to others today?

Today's key verse: "The wise in heart accept commands, but a chattering fool comes to ruin" (Proverbs 10:8).

Pray together: Show us, Lord, how to be wise in heart, accepting of your commands, and careful about foolish chattering.

Weekly memory verse: "Wisdom has built her house; she has set up its seven pillars" (Proverbs 9:1).

Shared Journal Experience: Turn to the Shared Journal Experience section for week 5, day 4, and share words of encouragement with each other.

Sandee Macgregor

SHARED JOURNAL EXPERIENCE

Week 5. Day 4

Mom

What character traits have you seen in your son that have blessed others. Select and write out a proverb of Solomon from Proverbs 10:1–16 to encourage your son today.

_____

_____

_____

_____

_____

_____

_____

_____

_____

_____

_____

_____

_____

_____

_____

_____

_____

_____

_____

_____

MEMORY VERSE

Wisdom has built her house;
she has set up its seven pillars.

(Proverbs 9:1)

SHARED JOURNAL EXPERIENCE

Week 5. Day 4

Son

Today's key verse reminds us that when you are "wise in your heart", you are more able to hear instructions from others. How has your mom influenced you to be "wise in your heart" (10:8)?

_____

_____

_____

_____

_____

_____

_____

_____

_____

_____

_____

_____

_____

_____

_____

_____

_____

_____

_____

_____

TODAY'S KEY VERSE

The wise in heart accept commands,
but a chattering fool comes to ruin.

(Proverbs 10:8)

WEEK 5

Day 5

Read together Proverbs 10:17–32.
Focus on and discuss Proverbs 10:17–24.

¹⁷ Whoever **heeds discipline** shows the **way to life**,
   but whoever **ignores correction** leads others **astray**.
¹⁸ Whoever conceals hatred with **lying lips**
   and spreads **slander** is a fool.
¹⁹ Sin is not ended by multiplying words,
   but the **prudent hold their tongues**.
²⁰ The **tongue of the righteous** is **choice silver**,
   but the heart of the wicked is of little value.
²¹ The lips of the righteous **nourish many**,
   but fools die for **lack of sense**.
²² **The blessing of the Lord** brings wealth,
   without painful toil for it.
²³ A fool finds pleasure in wicked schemes,
   but a person of understanding **delights in wisdom**.
²⁴ What the wicked dread will overtake them;
   what the **righteous desire** will be granted.

Discuss each of the highlighted words and phrases in this passage that lead us toward building a solid foundation in Christ. How can you walk in the way of insight today? How can your words and actions be a blessing to others today?

Today's key verse: "The tongue of the righteous is choice silver, but the heart of the wicked is of little value" (Proverbs 10:20).

Pray together: Lord, teach us to delight in your wisdom, and may our words be like choice silver that blesses others.

Weekly memory verse: "Wisdom has built her house; she has set up its seven pillars" (Proverbs 9:1).

Shared Journal Experience: Turn to the Shared Journal Experience section for week 5, day 5, and share words of encouragement with each other.

SHARED JOURNAL

Week 5. Day 5

Write the finish date of your journey: _____

Mom

Share with your son the gift Proverbs can be and ways it can stay close to his heart. Proverbs 10:23 says, "A fool finds pleasure in wicked schemes, but a person of understanding delights in wisdom." How can you and your son delight in wisdom together? Reflect on your time together over the past five weeks, and share what has been most meaningful.

_____
_____
_____
_____
_____
_____
_____
_____
_____
_____
_____
_____
_____
_____
_____

MEMORY VERSE

Wisdom has built her house;
she has set up its seven pillars.

(Proverbs 9:1)

SHARED JOURNAL EXPERIENCE

Week 5. Day 5

Write the finish date of your journey: _____

Son

Share some of your favourite parts of this journey studying Proverbs. Write down a special place you would like to go to with your mom and record where you go so you can look back and remember this special day!

_____
_____
_____
_____
_____
_____
_____
_____
_____
_____
_____
_____
_____
_____
_____
_____
_____
_____

TODAY'S KEY VERSE

The tongue of the righteous is choice silver,
but the heart of the wicked is of little value.

(Proverbs 10:20)

Day 5 – Ready, Set, Go

READY to be together

Proverbs 10:4 talks about lazy and diligent hands. Seek out some creative ways to serve with diligent hands, whether around your home, for your neighbours, or at church. Perhaps it's making a meal, delivering groceries, cleaning out a car, or doing yard work. After this, ask your son what he would like to do with you! Try to set time aside often to create space to build upon your relationship. Be willing to try something new, together.

SET your music to worship

"Sufficient for Me" (Jonathon Ogden)

"How Deep the Father's Love for Us" (Austin Stone Worship)

"For God Is With Us" (For King & Country)

"A Thousand Hallelujahs" (Brooke Ligertwood)

"I Speak Jesus" (Here Be Lions)

GO to read or listen to audiobooks or watch movies together

Listen or Watch

"Wisdom Videos" (BibleProject)

"Epic: An Around-the-World Journey through Christian History" (Tim Challies)

Read

The Radical Book for Kids: Exploring the Roots and Shoots of Faith (Champ Thornton)

The Wingfeather Saga (Andrew Petersen)

Just for Mom:

Fresh Joy (Heidi MacLaughlin)

Women of the Bible Small Group Bible Study (Marina Hofman)

Part 2

Resources

A Way to Remember Wisdom

The wisdom found in Proverbs is a firm foundation for our lives. Here is a way to remember and apply the wisdom of Proverbs with our sons.

L – Look up

Encourage wise mentors in your son's life

E – Engage

Encourage the gift of a church community

A – Ask

Encourage your son to ask questions

N – No compromise

Encourage the gift of godly character

I – Integrity matters

Encourage the importance of integrity

N – Next steps

Encourage setting goals and looking ahead

Three verses to memorize together

God is our sure foundation: "He will be the sure foundation for your times, a rich store of salvation and wisdom and knowledge; the fear of the Lord is the key to this treasure" (Isaiah 33:6).

God's Word stands firm: "Your word, Lord, is eternal; it stands firm in the heavens" (Psalm 119:89).

God sets our feet on the rock-solid truth: "I waited patiently for the Lord; he turned to me and heard my cry. He lifted me out of the slimy pit, out of the mud and mire; he set my feet on a rock and gave me a firm place to stand" (Psalm 40:1–2).

Milestone letter

Recently, my parents passed on a letter they wrote me during my third year of university. They found it in a box of old papers, and I am grateful they passed it along. I read through it and remembered just how special the words were for me at that time. I was close to finishing school and was struggling. They made a specific effort to share much-needed encouragement. I will keep that letter and remember for many more years their faithfulness as godly, encouraging, and loving parents.

Both my husband and I received from our parents through the years what I would call "milestone letters" to their children. These letters we received at different stages in our lives were filled with intentional words meant to encourage, inspire, gently convict, and impress upon the hearts of their kids a heavenly perspective layered in God's Word.

Today, consider writing a letter celebrating a milestone in your son's life. You decide the milestone! It could be graduation, learning to read, a sports/music/art achievement, a character award, baptism, or entering high school. It can be as simple and meaningful as celebrating he is a wonderful son, brother, friend, or grandson! There is *always* a reason to celebrate others. Sharing words of encouragement is a blessing that goes well beyond the pages written. Pray that the words will remain in his heart and that he will be able to draw on them in years to come to nourish the thirsty soul.

As you consider writing a milestone letter, pray over your son. I have a vivid memory of our family being seated around the dinner table and my parents asking each child to insert our names in the passage from 1 Corinthians 13:4–7. This is a practical way to pray, simply add his name where you see the blank line.

_____ is patient, _____ is kind. _____ does not envy_____, does not boast, _____ is not proud. _____ does not dishonor others, _____ is not self-seeking, _____ is not easily angered, _____ keeps no record of wrongs. _____ does not delight in evil but rejoices with the truth. _____ always protects, always trusts, always hopes, always perseveres.

Prayer of Protection

This passage from Ephesians 6:10–20 can be used as a powerful way to pray for protection over your son. Add his name to the spaces provided. Then, you can have your son pray this prayer over you and use your name in the spaces.

_____ be strong in the Lord and in his mighty power. Put on the full armor of God, so that you _____ can take your stand against the devil's schemes. For our struggle is not against flesh and blood, but against the rulers, against the authorities, against the powers of this dark world and against the spiritual forces of evil in the heavenly realms. Therefore _____ put on the full armor of God, so that when the day of evil comes, you may be able to stand your ground, and after you have done everything, to stand. Stand firm then, _____ with the belt of truth buckled around your waist, with the breastplate of righteousness in place, and with your feet _____ fitted with the readiness that comes from the gospel of peace. In addition to all this, take up the shield of faith, _____ with which you can extinguish all the flaming arrows of the evil one. Take the helmet of salvation_____ and the sword of the Spirit, _____ which is the word of God.

And pray in the Spirit _____ on all occasions with all kinds of prayers and requests. With this in mind, _____ be alert and always keep on praying for all the Lord's people. Pray also for me, that whenever I speak, words may be given me so that I will fearlessly make known the mystery of the gospel, for which I am an ambassador in chains. Pray that I may declare it fearlessly, as I should.

Milestone Letter For Your Son:

Leading Our Sons to Christ

I could not have orchestrated the day one of my kids came to me in tears and asked to pray together. What unfolded was a heartfelt prayer asking to be forgiven and thanking Jesus for his death on the cross and resurrection. We cried, hugged, and documented the event in a journal so we would not forget. I didn't set the time; God did!

The salvation of our sons is in God's perfect and capable hands. John 6:40 reminds us of this truth: "My Father's will is that everyone who looks to the Son and believes in him shall have eternal life, and I will raise them up at the last day." Further on, we read, "No one can come to me unless the Father who sent me draws them, and I will raise them up at the last day. (John 6:44) These verses remind us that we don't draw in our sons; God does, and we pray for their hearts to turn toward God. For ourselves, we rest in God's sovereignty and, with his help, radiate Christ.

It is the work of the Holy Spirit in the lives of our sons that changes their hearts. We diligently and consistently pray. A great place to begin is with the fact that we are all born sinners and in need of saving. In Romans 3:10, we are told, "As it is written: 'There is no one righteous, not even one,'" and Romans 3:23 says, "All have sinned and fall short of the glory of God." We are sinners, separated from God, "God demonstrates his own love for us in this: While we were still sinners, Christ died for us" (Romans 5:8). We help our sons understand that their (and our) sinful nature keeps them from a relationship with a holy God. God sent his Son to save us from our sins, and John 3:16 beautifully announces this truth: "God so loved the world that he gave his one and only Son, that whoever believes in him shall not perish but have eternal life."

Jesus died in our place, defeated death, and is preparing an eternal home for us, "My Father's house has many rooms; if that were not so, would I have told you that I am going there to prepare a place for you?" (John 14:2). Knowing that God was preparing a place for me was exciting when I was young; it still is today. This personal perspective was comforting and provided me with hope and anticipation of what was to come. It is good to know these truths, but we have to receive and respond to Christ's invitation to be forgiven. Understanding our sin and knowing that God sent his Son to die on the cross in our place and rise again on the third day leads us to receive Christ and trust him to forgive our sins. It is a gift that we respond to and receive! "If you declare with your mouth, 'Jesus is Lord,' and believe in your heart that God raised him from the dead, you will be saved" (Romans 10:9). It is a gift God gives us: "It is by grace you have been saved, through faith—and this is not from yourselves, it is the gift of God—not by works, so that no one can boast" (Ephesians 2:8–9).

If our son expresses a desire to receive Christ as his personal Saviour, we can share this prayer with him, similar to what I prayed many years ago: "Dear Jesus, I know I am a sinner. I need your forgiveness today. I believe you died on the cross in my place and rose from the grave. I know that you love me and have a plan for my life. Today, I receive your gift of eternal life and ask you to come into my heart and take the lead in my life. Amen."

Worship together:

"No Longer Slaves" (Zach Williams)

"Good Good Father" (Chris Tomlin and Pat Barrett)

"Who You Say I Am" (Hillsong Worship)

"This I Believe The Creed" (Hillsong Worship)

"Mercy" (Elevation Worship and Maverick City Worship)

Reading through Proverbs 11–31

Throughout the rest of Proverbs, read a few verses daily, perhaps mixed with a book from the New Testament. Highlight or underline verses as you go and pray the wisdom takes root in your heart and the hearts of those in your home.

It's easy to pray, speak out loud, or write wisdom for others, but it is an entirely different approach to accepting what God says to you. The challenge is to be open to the gentle working of the Spirit and receive the message of the life-giving gospel. Reading the Word will change us; we will become more like Jesus and model the importance of this habit of reading Scripture for our sons.

Studying one verse at a time, prayerful meditation, and thoughtfully writing down how the verse is shaping you will bring fruit that only God can beautifully display in your life. Read alone quietly and prepare to share openly with others how God is refreshing you!

We are reminded in Romans, "God's kindness is intended to lead you to repentance" (2:4) Each verse in Proverbs has the opportunity to lead us toward Christ and is overflowing with generous handfuls of truth for all areas of our lives. Wisdom calls out, "My fruit is better than fine gold; what I yield surpasses choice silver" (Proverbs 8:19). Through Proverbs, I pray that we will all hear the call of wisdom, set our minds on Christ (Colossian 3:2), and remember, "My dear brothers and sisters, stand firm. Let nothing move you. Always give yourselves fully to the work of the Lord, because you know that your labor in the Lord is not in vain" (1 Corinthians 15:58).

Sandee Macgregor

A Mother–Daughter
Devotional and
Shared Journal
Experience for
Psalm 119

CASTLE QUAY BOOKS

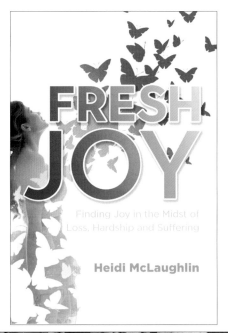

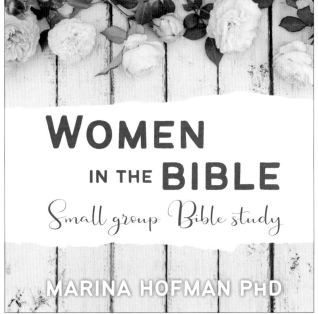

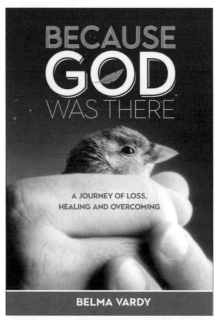

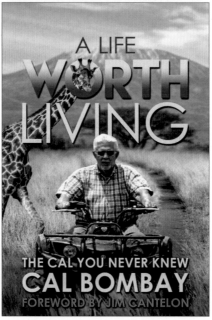